S0-DTG-344

THE DINOSAUR HUNTER'S HANDBOOK

Running Press
Philadelphia, Pennsylvania

Copyright © 1990 by Running Press
Printed in the United States of America. All rights reserved under the Pan-American and International Copyright Conventions.

This book may not be reproduced in whole or in part in any form or by any means, electronic or mechanical, including photocopying, recording, or by any information storage and retrieval system now known or hereafter invented, without written permission from the publisher.

Canadian representatives: General Publishing Co., Ltd., 30 Lesmill Road, Don Mills, Ontario M3B 2T6.

International representatives: Worldwide Media Services, Inc., 115 East Twenty-third Street, New York, New York 10010.

9   8   7   6   5   4   3

Digit on the right indicates the number of this printing.

Library of Congress Cataloging-in-Publication Number 89-43593

ISBN 0-89471-797-9

Editor: Steven Zorn
Text by Ted Daeschler

Package and book cover design by Toby Schmidt
Package front illustration adapted from *Ceratosaurus and Stegosaurus* by Bob Walters;
        © 1980 by Bob Walters
Package back illustration adapted from *Monster Dinosaurs* by Bob Walters; © 1982 by
        Bob Walters.
Package back photographs: (left) Courtesy of the Canadian Government Travel Bureau;
        (right) Courtesy of the Department of Library Services, American Museum of Natural
        History, neg. no. 337646.
Package photographs by Bel-Hop Studios, Belkowitz–Hopkins Photography

Book cover illustration: *Monster Dinosaurs* by Bob Walters; © 1980 by Bob Walters
Interior book design by Robert Perry
Interior book photographs: Courtesy of the Department of Library Services, American
        Museum of Natural History: p. 6, neg. no. 325277 (Photo by Rota); p. 9, neg. no.
        17506; p. 17, neg. no. 19488 (Photo by Brown); p. 19, neg. no. 329319 (Photo by
        Boltin); p. 20, neg. no. 45615; p. 21, neg. no. 310477 (Photo by H. S. Rice); p. 23,
        neg. no. 315713.
        Courtesy of the Field Museum of Natural History: p. 11, neg. no. 81443; p. 15,
        neg. no. 3934; p. 18, neg. no. 3251.
        UPI/Bettmann Newsphotos: pp. 13, 22.
        U.S. Geological Survey: p. 14 (Photo by W. R. Hansen).
Interior book illustrations: Christine Colligan: title page, p. 5, 25, 37, 49.
        Bob Walters: pp. 10, 27–31, 34, 35 © 1985; p. 26 © 1986; pp. 32, 33 © 1987.
Calligraphy by Judith Barbour Osborne

Typography by Commcor Communications Corporation, Philadelphia, Pennsylvania

This book may be ordered by mail from the publisher.
Please add $2.50 for postage and handling.
But try your bookstore first!
Running Press Book Publishers
125 South Twenty-second Street
Philadelphia, Pennsylvania 19103

CONTENTS

PART ONE

On The Trail
Of
Dinosaurs

No one has ever seen a living dinosaur. The last of these astounding creatures vanished more than 60 million years before the first humans evolved. How is it that we know so much about animals that lived so long ago?

It's taken nearly 200 years and the work of thousands of scientists to solve some of the mysteries and piece together what we know about dinosaurs. Scientists are still trying to answer many questions, so

Triceratops skull, about 70 million years old

now is an exciting time to be a dinosaur hunter.

Dinosaur hunters are called paleontologists. They work outdoors where they dig for fossil bones, teeth, footprints, and even impressions of skin in ancient rocks. Paleontologists also work in scientific laboratories where fossils are repaired and then studied.

This book and kit will show you how we've learned about dinosaurs, and how dinosaur paleontologists do their work. The most important traits of a fossil hunter are patience and carefulness, so take your time as you read this book and as you work on the model dinosaur skeleton included in this kit. With this kit, you can experience the excitement of discovering your own dinosaur fossils.

A New Science

A little more than 200 years ago, no one even dreamed that animals such as dinosaurs once lived. When the fossil bones and teeth of dinosaurs were first discovered in England in the 1700s, some people thought they were the remains of giant men that they had heard about in legends. Scientists, however, searched for a better explanation.

Late in the 1700s, a Frenchman named George Cuvier compared the fossil bones and teeth found in England with the bones and teeth of living animals. To his astonishment, he discovered that the huge bones found in England were the remains of reptiles. These reptiles were similar to lizards but different from any known kind. There wasn't an official name for these creatures until 1841, when British scientist Sir Richard Owen called them *dinosaurs,* which means "terrible reptiles."

Dinosaur bones were later discovered in Montana in 1855. The western part of North America is one of the best areas on earth to hunt dinosaur fossils. This is because of the kinds of rocks that make up that part of the continent. Dinosaur fossils are most often found in rocks formed from layers of sand and mud that were carried by streams during the Age of Reptiles, also called the Mesozoic Era, between 250 and 65 million years ago. These rocks are common in the western United States and Canada.

Some of the earliest and most important dinosaur fossils were discovered by William Parker Foulke in 1858. They were found along the east coast of North America, at Haddonfield, New Jersey. From these fossils, Dr. Joseph Leidy was able to accurately reconstruct the skeleton and posture of a duck-billed

Mounting the forelimbs of a *Brontosaurus (Apatosaurus)*
at the American Museum of Natural History, New York, 1904

dinosaur that he named *Hadrosaurus foulkii,* which means "Foulke's big reptile." At the time, it was the most complete dinosaur skeleton found anywhere in the world.

During the last half of the 1800s, American settlers started moving west to explore the new frontier. Fossil hunters weren't far behind. In the 1870s and 1880s, an intense rivalry developed between Othniel C. Marsh of New Haven, Connecticut, and Edward Drinker Cope of Philadelphia. Each man hired many workers and competed to discover and name new dinosaurs.

In the early 1900s, many excellent dinosaur fossils were collected in Alberta, Canada, and in China. The American Museum of Natural History in New York sent an expedition to central Asia which led to some important discoveries, including 25 *Protoceratops* eggs—the first dinosaur eggs ever unearthed.

In this century, new discoveries have been made by workers from many countries. New kinds of dinosaurs are often unearthed, and older collections are being re-studied.

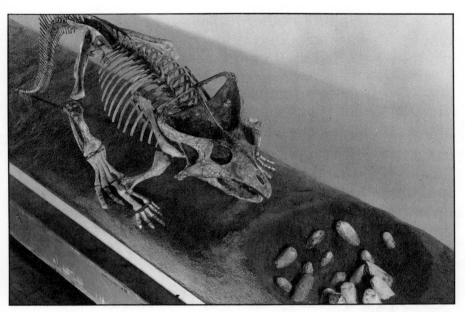

A *Protoceratops*
and her eggs

More Questions than Answers

Did you ever wonder how many kinds of dinosaurs there were? What colors they were? What sounds they made? Paleontologists wonder about these things, too, and they are still trying to find answers. Paleontologists are asking other questions as well: How are dinosaurs related to other reptiles and to birds? Were dinosaurs warm-blooded? How did they move? What did they eat? Did they care for their young?

Recently, paleontologists have found new evidence that some dinosaurs traveled in herds. They've also noticed similarities between dinosaurs found in China's Gobi Desert and the dinosaurs found in Canada. This discovery suggests that there may have been a land bridge linking Asia and North America millions of years ago. Each discovery gives us another piece in the puzzle of our understanding of dinosaurs and our planet.

Collecting Dinosaurs: A Step-by-Step Guide

Can you imagine how much work it takes to dig up a 40-foot-long dinosaur skeleton from the rock where it's buried, then transport it, clean it, and repair it so that it can be studied? It might take months, and it also takes a scientific mind and a strong back.

Most dinosaur collecting is done by paleontologists who work at universities and museums which sponsor research trips. If you're a paleontologist who wants to dig for dinosaur fossils, the first step is to

Excavating bones on a farm in Indiana

read as much as possible about the area you'll be exploring. It helps to know what to expect, and to learn from the experiences of others.

Next is the planning stage: maps and equipment are checked and a plan of action is made for the days or weeks ahead. Areas where dinosaur fossils are found are often far from towns, so careful planning of food and other supplies leaves more time for fossil hunting once you reach the site.

Usually, dinosaur hunters camp out. They sleep in tents and have no running water or electricity. In the summer, when most paleontologists do their outdoor work (they call it "field work"), the nights are warm and the days are long. Hot weather, insects, rain, wind, and the sore muscles that come from hard work are the only annoyances that paleontologists must put up with—but most dinosaur hunters are too busy to mind.

Once you reach the area you want to explore, you begin the search for fossils by prospecting. To prospect, slowly walk along the bases of cliffs, along hillsides, or in drainages, looking on the ground for fragments of fossils that have washed out of the rock.

A paleontologist carefully chips the rock from a dinosaur backbone in a quarry in Utah.

Once you spot fossil fragments, look around to try and find where they came from. If you're patient—and lucky—you can find the layer of rock that the fragment washed out of, and maybe you'll find other fossils still buried there. Fossils that are buried will be in good condition. Sometimes a dinosaur paleontologist can prospect all day, and find nothing but a few fragments. Patience is important; tomorrow may be a lucky day.

Whan you do find dinosaur fossils, they will probably be only pieces of a skeleton. Rarely are all the bones of a dinosaur found together. That's because when any animal dies, other animals scatter the bones or carry them off as they scavenge for food. A skeleton that isn't quickly buried is destroyed by sun and rain. A skeleton that gets washed into a stream will usually fall apart, and some parts will wash away as others are buried.

A single dinosaur bone can be an impressive find.

Make a Note of It

Whether or not you find fossils, it's important to *keep notes* about where you've been and what you've found. These notes are called "field notes." They're like a journal in which you write down details of your dinosaur hunt. They supply important information to you and other scientists in the future.

Your field notes should include the following:

- where you're exploring
- the date and time
- a description of the rocks you're digging (note whether they are hard or soft, dark or light)
- a simple map of the area
- a description and sketches of the fossils you've found
- the field numbers of the fossils you've found (more about this on page 19).

You'll find sample field notes in Section 2 of this book, and you'll have a chance to write your own notes in Section 3 as you dig your own dinosaur.

Bringing 'em Home

Once you've found part of a dinosaur skeleton and made complete notes, you must carefully excavate and remove it. A fossil that has been buried for millions of years is usually very fragile. Using tools such as a wood awl or ice pick, geologic hammer, trowel, brushes, and chisels, carefully clear the rock from the top surface of the fossil. This may take a few

A jacketed fossil is carefully hoisted
out of the ground in Canada, 1914.

minutes or a few days, depending upon the size of the
fossil and the hardness of the rock where it's buried.
(You may need the help of an assistant.)

After you have uncovered the fossil and you
know its size and shape, dig a trench into the rock
around it. The trench should be about two inches
from the fossil's edges so that the specimen is sitting
on a pedestal.

The next step is called jacketing the specimen. Completely cover the fossil with wet paper towels or toilet paper, then wrap it with strips of burlap that have been soaked in plaster.

The plaster jacket takes several hours to dry. When it's ready, deepen the trench around the fossil and begin to dig beneath it. Eventually, you'll be able to roll over the plaster-covered bundle. Cover the bottom of the fossil with more plaster-soaked burlap. Once dry, the fossil and rock are safely enclosed in a rigid case.

Putting dinosaur bones together again is a delicate task.

Coelophysis fossils, discovered in New Mexico

Keeping Track

It's hard to tell fossils apart when they're wrapped up like mummies, so you should be sure to label each fossil case as soon as possible.

You can use any system you like to label your fossil, but one of the most convenient ways is to give it a "field number." Your field number could include the date and a three-digit number. For example, if you found your first fossil in 1990, your field label could read "90–001." A fossil with the label "90–045" means that this was the 45th fossil you found in 1990. Don't forget to write the field number in your field notes along with the rest of the identifying information. Now the fossil can be brought to the laboratory.

Dinosaurs in the Lab

In the laboratory, the fossil must be repaired and preserved.

The first step is to cut open the plaster jacket around the fossil. Once the top half of the jacket is removed, you can begin to carefully chip away the rock that was left around the fossil. Tools for this job vary from hammer and chisel to dental picks and pins used under a microscope.

Applying the finishing touches
to an *Apatosaurus* fossil

Sometimes a dinosaur fossil is in hundreds of pieces. Each piece must be cleaned and glued together like a puzzle. This can take many hours of work, but the result can be a magnificent fossil that will add to your knowledge about dinosaurs.

The last step is to put the fossil on display or, more often, add it to a research collection at a university or museum where it can be studied. The museum or university will give your fossil a catalog number, which is written in ink right on the fossil. Every museum and university has its own system for making up catalog numbers. Besides being written on the fossil, the catalog number is also recorded in a ledger book and on a computer, along with other important information such as where the fossil was collected, what rock formation it came from, who collected it, when it was collected, and how it was prepared. The museum or university will also keep your field notes so that scientists may study them years later.

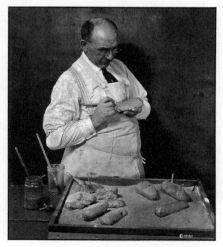

From eggs like these sprang mighty dinosaurs.

Hitting the Books

Once a fossil has been restored and cataloged, you can begin to examine it. What parts of the skeleton do you have? What kind of dinosaur is it? How do the bones fit together? The answers to these questions are usually found by reading and studying in a science library.

Scientist David Weishampel holds a model of a dinosaur nasal passage, through which he believes dinosaurs made honking sounds.

Paleontologists identify fossils by comparing them with living creatures and with fossils that have already been identified. This technique is called *comparative anatomy.* Many scientists have drawn the fossils that they discovered. These descriptions and drawings are found in thousands of books that paleontologists must use often.

To learn about fossils, we can compare them with living animals.

For example, the long neck and grinding teeth of some dinosaurs suggest that they ate leaves or needles from tall trees, as giraffes do. A dinosaur with claws and sharp teeth certainly ate meat, as a lion does. The feet of some dinosaurs look like the feet of large birds, such as the ostrich, which suggests that some dinosaurs could run like ostriches.

Through these processes of discovery, collection, preparation, and study, paleontologists gathered many fossils and learned a lot about the dinosaurs. Still, there's no doubt much, much more to learn.

A model of the *Styracosaurus* at the American Museum of Natural History

PART TWO

How Dinosaurs Get Their Names

The word "dinosaur" comes from the Greek word *deinos,* meaning "terrible," and the Latin word *saurus,* which means "reptile." Since dinosaurs, because of their enormous size, were so frightening, "terrible reptile" seemed like a good name for these creatures.

Scientists use Latin and Greek words to name dinosaurs according to some feature of the animal. Once you know what the words mean, it's easy to imagine what the dinosaur looked like. Here are some dinosaur names and their meanings:

HADROSAURUS

Hadrosaurus (hadro =big, *saurus* =reptile): big reptile
Hadrosaurus was a duck-billed, plant-eating
dinosaur. The discovery of its fossilized skeleton in
New Jersey in 1858 provided convincing evidence that
dinosaurs could stand upright.

TRICERATOPS

Triceratops (*tri*=three, *cera*=horn, *tops*=face): three-horned face

    Triceratops is the best-known of the horned dinosaurs and one of the last dinosaurs to walk the earth. *Triceratops* was a plant-eater that used its horns to defend itself against enemies.

PACHYCEPHALOSAURUS

Pachycephalosaurus (*pachy*=thick, *cephalo*=head):
thick-headed reptile

The skull of the *Pachycephalosaurus* was about 9 inches thick. Males probably competed for territory or mates by banging heads with one another.

29

DEINONYCHUS

Deinonychus (*deino* =terrible, *nychus* =claw): terrible claw

A gruesome killing machine, *Deinonychus* would tightly hold its prey and kick it to death using the sharp claws on its feet.

TYRANNOSAURUS

Tyrannosaurus (*tyranno*=tyrant): tyrant reptile
   Tyrannosaurus rex, the king of the tyrant lizards,
measured more than 40 feet long, weighed about 8
tons, and had teeth up to 6 inches long.

STRUTHIOMIMUS

Struthiomimus (*struthio*=ostrich, *mimus*=mimic):
ostrich-mimic

    Struthiomimus stood about 10 feet tall. With its
small head, long legs, and long neck, this dinosaur
looked like an ostrich and was probably an equally
fast runner.

IGUANODON

Iguanodon (iguano=iguana, *don*=tooth): iguana-tooth
　　An iguana is a type of reptile. The teeth of this
dinosaur look like the teeth of the iguana.

MAIASAURA

Maiasaura (*maia*=good mother): good mother reptile
   Adult maiasaurs were discovered in nesting
grounds complete with eggs and young dinosaurs.
This proved that maiasaurs took care of their young.

Apatosaurus

Apatosaurus (*apato*=deceptive): deceptive reptile
   Apatosaurus used to be called *Brontosaurus* ("thunder reptile"). Its name was changed when scientists discovered that *Brontosaurus* was put together using parts from different dinosaurs! When the dinosaur was assembled properly, it was renamed *Apatosaurus*.

PART THREE

A
Fossil Hunter's
Notebook

Monday, 6/25

12:30 p.m. — We were up with the sun (as usual) this morning. Had a big break-fast and met to work out the day's plan. We split into 2 groups. My group (3 of us) spent the a.m. exploring an area 4 miles S.W. of our campsite, along a creek which has cut a small valley. Group #2 went to work on the hadrosaur bones that we found yesterday in the bad-lands 5-6 miles S. of camp.

We were on our way by 8 a.m. The terrain is rough here,

and at times our 4-wheel almost slipped off the road. We stopped when we could go no further and filled our day packs with water, lunch, maps, tools and other collecting gear. Then we hiked to the top of a small hill to survey the area.

This part of Montana is called the high plains for good reason. The Rocky Mountains are not far to the west, but all around us the ground is flat prairie, interrupted by areas where erosion has stripped away the soil and exposed soft rock beneath. Perfect fossil-hunting grounds!

It's hard to imagine how different this whole territory looked 75 million years ago when the dinosaurs lived here. Streams from the west flowed east into a wide, shallow seaway that covered the center of what's now North America. Dinosaur bones were occasionally buried in the sandy streams. Today we're digging in the rocky bottoms of those ancient streams that form a window into the past for fossil hunters.

From the hilltop we surveyed the area of badlands that we wanted to explore. (This area is in the N.W. corner of Section 32 on the map of the Mount Moro Quadrangle.) Sedimentary rock is exposed in 2 streams that flow S. We'd never hunted for fossils here before, so we began by prospecting. We began at the base of a small hill with two tilted rocks on top (see map), and headed into the badlands and examined most of the area in about $1\frac{1}{2}$ hours. Found no sign of fossils except at one spot, where we found fragments of a turtle shell (field # 90-032).

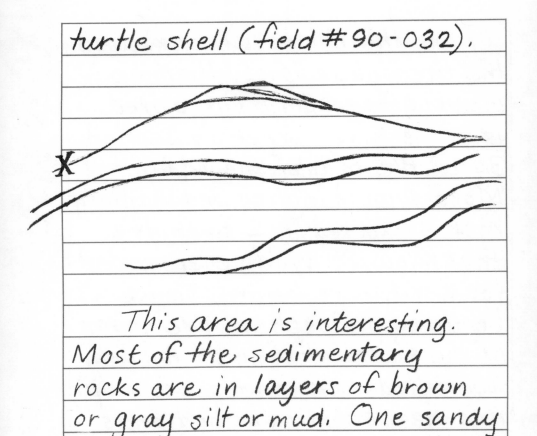

X

This area is interesting. Most of the sedimentary rocks are in layers of brown or gray silt or mud. One sandy channel shows a stream that flowed E-W.

Lunch time — We're relaxing in the shade of a lone tree. This afternoon we'll join crew #2.

5:30 p.m. — After lunch we helped group #2 with the hadrosaur bones discovered yesterday. (see notes of 6/23 for exact location.) The bones are buried in a light-colored, sandy layer of rock. I collected small bits of petrified wood and a few leaf impressions from nearby in the same layer (field #90-033).
By the time we arrived,

the others had already cleared the sandy rock away from the bones and uncovered an upper arm bone, a shoulder blade, and three pieces of rib (diagram below).

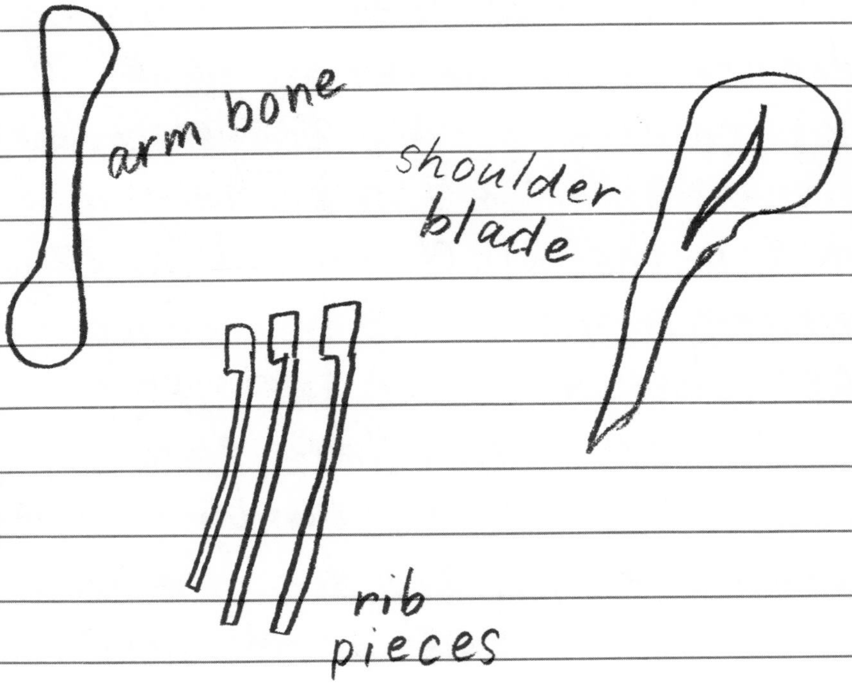

arm bone

shoulder blade

rib pieces

The bones were separated from each other by 1-2 feet, but they probably belonged to the same dinosaur.

It was a bit crowded with 6 of us working at the same site, but the work of digging trenches around the bones went quickly. We covered the bones with wet paper towel, mixed the plaster, and quickly wrapped the bones in burlap and plaster bandages.

It was getting late so we decided to let the plaster dry overnight and explore the area nearby. We split up to prospect.

After about 15 minutes I heard an excited yell from over a hill. When I found where it came from, 4 of the others were on their knees carefully brushing sand away from something.

As I got closer, I could see dinosaur teeth on the surface. Still closer, I saw part of a dinosaur's jaw sticking out of the rock. An exciting find! We didn't have time to collect the jaw today, so we covered it with plastic and then a layer of sand. We sketched and photographed the site. Then we collected all the pieces on the surface (field #90-034), marked the spot with a pile of stones, and marked our field map with a star.

The jaw looks very interesting. I'm not sure what kind of dinosaur it is, but judging from the teeth, it's definitely one of the plant eaters.

Tomorrow is going to be exciting!

PART FOUR

Dig
Your Own
Apatosaurus

A*patosaurus* ("deceptive reptile") lived from 150 to 135 million years ago. Its fossils have been found in Colorado, Wyoming, Oklahoma, and Utah. Although this dinosaur is traditionally called *Brontosaurus,* its correct scientific name is *Apatosaurus*. This plant-eater was 70 feet long, 15 feet tall at the shoulders, and weighed 30 tons. Despite its tremendous size, *Apatosaurus* had a brain about the size of a cat's.

Like a giraffe, *Apatosaurus* probably ate the leaves of tall trees. It swallowed these leaves whole, and they were ground up by stones that *Apatosaurus* swallowed for this purpose. *Apatosaurus* had weak jaws and few teeth.

Fossilized tracks show that *Apatosaurus* sometimes traveled in herds. Younger dinosaurs walked in the center of the herd where they were safe from meat-eating dinosaurs. No dragging tail marks have been found with *Apatosaurus* footprints, so it seems that these dinosaurs walked with their tails raised.

Getting Ready

Your dinosaur kit contains a replica of an *Apatosaurus* skeleton buried in hard, slate-like layers and covered with clay-like rock similar to the soft rocks where real fossils are found.

To uncover the dinosaur skeleton, scrape away the soft rock, being careful not to damage the skeleton underneath.

A wooden spatula is included in your kit to use in scraping away the rock. You can use the spatula just as it is, or you may want to sharpen it by rubbing its edge against the pavement. You may also want to use other tools such as **a plastic knife**, **a stiff toothbrush**, and **toothpicks**.

You'll also need **a bucket of water** to soften the outer layer of rock and to clean your newly-discovered fossil pieces.

Fossil hunting is *messy!* Paleontologists work outdoors, so you may want to take your dinosaur kit outside to work on. If you're going to stay indoors, be sure to cover your work area with plenty of **newspapers.** Keep **paper towels** nearby to wipe your hands, and wear old clothes.

Fossils break very easily, and so can the dinosaur in your kit. To prevent breakage, work carefully and *very slowly.* Don't feel badly if some of the pieces break or are missing—dinosaur hunters almost never find complete skeletons.

The pieces of your *Apatosaurus* fit together like a puzzle. Once you unearth the pieces, you'll glue them together with **white glue** (such as Elmer's Glue-All) to reconstruct the dinosaur. Use the watercolors provided to paint your *Apatosaurus*, and then you can polish it with **black shoe polish**. When you're done, your *Apatosaurus* will be ready for display.

The next few pages will lead you step by step through your dinosaur dig. There's plenty of space to write your observations and draw pictures of what you discover along the way. When you're done, you'll have a terrific dinosaur specimen and a complete set of personal field notes to document your find.

Field Notes from a Dinosaur Dig

Name:_____

(Assistant's Name: _____)

Date: _____

Location: _____

Beginning Time: _____

1 Unwrap the slab of rock and examine it. (Don't worry if the slab is broken into pieces—that makes your dig more realistic!)

Is any part of a dinosaur showing through the rock? Can you see what part it is? Draw a picture of it or describe it here:

2 Soak the slab in a bucket of water for at least 5 minutes to soften it.
What happened?

_____

_____

_____

_____

_____

_____

_____

_____

_____

_____

_____

_____

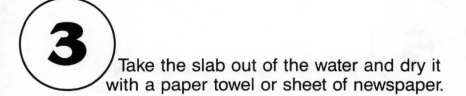

3 Take the slab out of the water and dry it with a paper towel or sheet of newspaper.

4 Now you're ready to start digging.
Use the wooden spatula included with your kit to scrape off the outer layer of clay. You may also want to try using a plastic knife for scraping.

Take your time! It's best to slide and scrape the spatula over the clay rather than jabbing or poking it. Remember: Dinosaur hunting is gentle work.

Occasionally dip the slab into the bucket of water to clear away the loosened clay. Remove all the clay from one side of the slab; then turn it over and start digging from the other side. (If you have to interrupt your dig, that's OK—just re-soak the slab in water before starting again.)

5 What does the clay feel like? Are you using hard pressure or light pressure? What tools are you using?
Describe what you're doing.

_____

_____

_____

_____

_____

_____

_____

_____

_____

_____

_____

_____

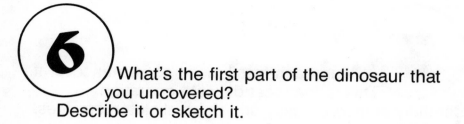

6 What's the first part of the dinosaur that you uncovered? Describe it or sketch it.

7 Clean each fossil piece as you uncover it. This is the most delicate operation. Carefully scrape the clay out of the skeleton crevices. Use toothpicks and a stiff toothbrush.

Dip the piece often into the bucket of water to wash away the loosened clay.

8 As you excavate each fossil piece, trace its shape on the blank page at the back of this book. (Use extra paper if you like.) Draw in its details.

You can also make *fossil rubbings.* Here's how: Place each fragment underneath a blank page and rub the page lightly with the side of a pencil lead or piece of charcoal. Use the lightest pressure possible. The shape of the fossil, along with all its bumps and dents, will print through the paper.

A sample fossil rubbing

9 Write a field number beneath each fossil tracing or rubbing and write the same number on the back of the actual fragment. (See page 19 for tips on writing field numbers.)

As you put the dinosaur skeleton together, you'll begin to recognize which fossil fragments form the dinosaur's ribs, which ones form its legs, and so forth. List the field numbers below along with the name of each piece as you identify it:

FIELD NUMBER:	DATE FOUND:	DESCRIPTION:
_____	_____	_____
_____	_____	_____
_____	_____	_____
_____	_____	_____
_____	_____	_____
_____	_____	_____
_____	_____	_____
_____	_____	_____

FIELD NUMBER: **DATE FOUND:**   **DESCRIPTION:**

FIELD NUMBER:	DATE FOUND:	DESCRIPTION:
_____	_____	_____
_____	_____	_____
_____	_____	_____
_____	_____	_____
_____	_____	_____

10 After you've excavated and cleaned all the fossil fragments, fit them together to construct the whole dinosaur.

The pieces should fit together exactly, but you must dry them thoroughly before you glue the *Apatosaurus* together.

11 Ask a grownup to be your lab assistant. Your assistant's job is to set the oven to 200°F and let the fossil pieces dry until their color has changed from black to gray (about an hour).

12 While the pieces are drying, prepare a work surface to construct your dinosaur. Lay some newspaper over a tabletop and place a plastic bag over it.

13 When the pieces are dry, place them on the plastic bag and begin to fit them together. Apply white glue to the edge of one piece where it meets another piece. Press the pieces together for a minute. Wipe the extra glue from the front side as you go.

Continue gluing the pieces together until the *Apatosaurus* is complete.

14 Wait an hour for the glue to dry, then turn the *Apatosaurus* over and remove the plastic bag.

Apply more glue to the cracks on the back side, and let the fossil dry for another hour.

15 Scrape off some of the gray rock from the back of the slab, mix the powder with an equal amount of white glue, and carefully fill any remaining cracks or holes on the front side.

If some of the bones are damaged or incomplete, you can repair them with the same mixture.

16 Paint the slab with black watercolor, and the bones with brown watercolor.
Let the paint dry for an hour.

17 Carefully apply black shoe polish to the whole slab, including the bones. Let it dry for 15 minutes.
Polish gently with a paper towel or soft brush.

Your *Apatosaurus* is now complete! You may want to make a fossil rubbing of the entire slab. (Follow the instructions in Step 8.)

Record the date and time you completed your dinosaur reconstruction:

DATE
COMPLETED:_____

TIME
COMPLETED:_____

If you want to display your *Apatosaurus,* have your grownup assistant drill four small holes into the slab about 1″ from each corner. Use small black nails or screws to mount the slab on a piece of wood. You can then hang the mounted slab on a wall, or display it on a shelf.

Write additional notes on your dig. What did you discover during the project?
What problems did you encounter and how did you solve them?

_____

_____

_____

_____

_____

_____

_____